PA SPORT

China

2nd Edition

Passport to the World

Passport Argentina
Passport Brazil
Passport China
Passport France
Passport Germany
Passport Hong Kong
Passport India
Passport Indonesia
Passport Israel
Passport Italy
Passport Japan
Passport Korea
Passport Mexico
Passport Philippines
Passport Poland
Passport Russia
Passport Singapore
Passport South Africa
Passport Spain
Passport Switzerland
Passport Taiwan
Passport Thailand
Passport United Kingdom
Passport USA
Passport Vietnam

PASSPORT
China

Your Pocket Guide to Chinese Business, Customs & Etiquette

2nd Edition

Jenny Li

Passport Series Editor: Barbara Szerlip

WORLD TRADE PRESS®
Books and E-Content for International Trade

World Trade Press
1450 Grant Avenue, Suite 204
Novato, California 94945 USA
Tel: +1 (415) 898-1124; Fax: +1 (415) 898-1080
USA Order Line: +1 (800) 833-8586
E-mail: sales@worldtradepress.com
www.worldtradepress.com
www.worldtraderef.com
www.globalroadwarrior.com
www.howtoconnect.com

Passport China, 2nd Edition
ISBN 1-885073-89-5
"Passport to the World" concept: Edward Hinkelman
Cover design: Peter Jones
Illustrations: Tom Watson

Disclaimer
This publication is designed to provide general information
concerning the cultural aspects of doing business with people
from a particular country. It is sold with the understanding that
the publisher is not engaged in rendering legal or any other professional services. If legal advice or other expert assistance is
required, the services of a competent professional person
should be sought.

Library of Congress Cataloging-in-Publication Data
Li, Jenny, 1953-
Passport China : your pocket guide to Chinese business, cus-
toms & etiquette / Jenny Li.--2nd ed.
p. cm. -- (Passport series)
ISBN 1-885073-89-5
1. Corporate culture -- China. 2. Business etiquette -- China. 3.
Industrial management -- Social aspects -- China. 4. Negotia-
tion in business -- China. 5. Intercultural communication.
I. Title II. Passport to the world.
HD58.7.L497 2003
390'.00951 -- dc21
2003042297
CIP

Printed in the United States of America

Table of Contents
China

The Middle Kingdom

1 Doing Business Across Cultures

Although business operations around the world have become highly standardized, national traditions, attitudes and beliefs remain diverse. Public praise, for example, is much enjoyed by its recipient in the U.S. and Europe, but is a source of embarrassment and discomfort for an individual in Asia. This is because Western cultures value individual thought and action, while Eastern cultures prize modesty and group consensus. In Asia, "the nail that sticks up gets hammered down."

While the primary focus of people in one culture might be to quickly get down to business, another culture concentrates first on developing personal relationships. Although their objectives may be the same, people from different cultures are likely to have very different ways of achieving them.

You'll probably never know a particular culture as well as your own — not only is the language different, but the historical context within which its people operate if often misunderstood by outsiders. When cultures collide, as they inevitably will, the damage can be greatly reduced by an appreciation of what caused the collision.

Comparing Values Across Cultures

One Culture:	Another Culture:
Values change	Values tradition
Favors specific communication	Favors ambiguous communication
Values analytical, linear problem solving	Values intuitive, lateral problem solving
Places emphasis on individual performance	Places emphasis on group performance
Considers verbal communication most important	Considers context & nonverbal communication most important
Focuses on task and product	Focuses on relationship and process
Places emphasis on promoting differing views	Places emphasis on harmony and consensus
Emphasizes competition	Emphasizes collaboration
Prefers informal tone	Prefers formal tone
Is flexible about schedules	Emphasizes rigid adherence to schedule

Passport China will offer some insights into the country and its people and help you understand how their traditions, values, business practices and communication styles differ from your own.

CHINA
Quick Look

Official name	People's Republic of China
Land area	9,326,410 sq. km.
Capital	Beijing (13,820,000)
Largest city	Shanghai (16,740,000)
Elevations	Highest – Zhu Mu Lang Ma (Mt. Everest) 8,843 m
	Lowest –Turpan Pendi 154 m

People

Population	1,284,303 (2002 est.)
Density	325 persons per sq. km.
Distribution	30% urban, 70% rural
Annual growth	0.87%
Official language	Mandarin
Major religions	Officially atheist; Buddhism and Taoism are traditional

Economy

GDP (2002)	US$5.56 trillion
	US$4,300 per capita
Foreign trade (2002)	Imports—US$236.2 billion
	Exports—US$262.1 billion
Principal trade partners	Hong Kong
	Japan, Taiwan,
	USA, South Korea
	Germany
Currency	Yuan (Y1=100 fen)
Exchange	Y8.27=US$1.00 (2002)

Education and health

Literacy	81.5% (2002)
Universities	212 (2002)
Hospital beds	1 per 420 persons
Physicians	1 per 595persons
Life expectancy	Women—73.86 years
	Men—70.02 years
Infant mortality	27.25 per 1,000 live births

CHINA

2 Country Facts

Geography and Demographics

Rooster-shaped China is the second largest country in the world, somewhat larger than third-ranked United States and smaller only than Canada. China stretches approximately 4,022 kilometers (2,500 miles) from the Pamir Mountains in the West to the East China Sea, about the distance from Paris to Teheran. From its southern border with Vietnam to its northern border with Russia is 3,218 kilometers (2,000 miles), the air distance between Manhattan and Mexico City. The Yangtze River (*Chang Jiang*), the longest river in China (6,336 kilometers/3,938 miles) and the third longest in the world, divides the country into two distinctive regions, North and South.

Mountains, plateaus and deserts cover two thirds of the country. So 90 percent of China's population lives on the 15 percent of the land that can be cultivated. The majority make their homes in the provinces along the country's 11,250 miles of coastline.

Approximately 93 percent of the people are Han Chinese. The remaining 83 million, members of China's 55 other ethnic groups, live mostly in the border regions. The Han Chinese first built their civilization four thousand years ago in the Yellow River (*Huang He*) valley, near what are today Henan and Shandong provinces. The 3,413-mile-long Yellow River, also called "the cradle of Chinese civilization," is the country's second longest. Ancient Han Chinese believed they lived at the center of the earth, thus the name China, which literally means "the Middle Kingdom."

China shares its borders with over a dozen neighboring countries, including India, Mongolia, North Korea, Pakistan, Russia and Vietnam. The central government in Beijing administrates 22 provinces, 5 autonomous regions and 3 cities (Beijing, Shanghai and Tianjin).

Climate

With such a vast area (49 degrees of latitude from north to south) and varied topography, China's climate ranges from sub-arctic to tropical. The country's two major climates are separated by the Yangtze River.

Winter in northern China usually starts in early November and continues through late March. Although dry and generally sunny, temperatures rarely rise above 0° C (32° F). Summer is hot, with temperatures reaching as high as 38° C (100° F). But with low humidity, the North is not as uncomfortable as some southern areas. July and August are the rainy months in the Beijing area, with frequent thunderstorms and showers.

Southern winters are shorter than southern summers, but very cold and humid (except in some very far southern areas such as Yunnan, Hainan and Guangdong). Temperatures can drop to –10° C (14° F). Snow is not unusual in some areas, including Shanghai, China's largest city. The summers are long, uncomfortably hot and humid, with temperatures above 38° C (100° F) for days at a time during July and August. Three of China's four "great ovens" — Nanjing, Wuhan and Chongqing — are in this area. The rainy season is from May to June, and even when it doesn't rain, the humidity remains high.

National Holidays

New Year*................................	January 1–3
Western (Solar) New Year*	January 1
Spring Festival	First, second and
(also known as the	third days
Chinese/Lunar New Year)	of first month of new
	lunar new year,
	usually February
International Women's Day** ...	March 8
International Labor Day*	May 1
International Children's Day***.	June 1
National Day*	October 1,2

* Paid legal holiday
** Female employees usually receive a paid half day off.
*** Parents who have only one child usually receive a paid half day off.

Although there are only six paid holidays in the country, many companies close their doors for a week during the Chinese New Year. They are typically open on the weekend immediately before the holiday and closed on the day immediately after so that employees will have an extra day off. No religious holidays are officially observed in China.

An interesting holiday is the Mid-Autumn or Moon Festival, (the 15th day of the eighth lunar month). Families gather for a big dinner that features special moon cakes filled with sweet red bean or lotus seed paste, and houses are decorated with rabbit-shaped lanterns. (An ancient story tells of a princess who lived in the Moon Palace with her pet rabbit.)

The Dragon Boat Festival (the fifth day of the fifth lunar month) commemorates Qu Yuan (340–278 B.C.), a poet and statesman who threw himself in the Miluo River to protest against corruption. Rice wrapped in bamboo leaves (originally thrown into the river to keep the fish from eating the drowned Qu Yuan's flesh) are a special treat, and teams race long, narrow river boats with a dragon's head carved into the bow.

December 22 of the solar calendar is the Winter Festival, which in the past was considered as important as New Year. Today, it is essentially a family affair. Restaurants and stores close early, and everyone eats round dumplings, since the circular shape symbolizes a never-ending relationship.

Business Hours

Effective May 1, 1995 — International Labor Day in China — the work week officially changed from six days to five. For most civil servants, a work day means 8 A.M. to 5 P.M. — with a lunch break from noon to 1:30, when most banks, government and business offices shut down, so that employees may go home for lunch and a *xiuxi* (a short nap). Shops and restaurants set their own hours, and these vary greatly.

Daily schedules change both seasonally and from region to region. For example, lunch breaks typically last longer during the summer months, with closing time pushed back accordingly (thus taking advantage of the longer daylight hours). Although China spans six time zones, there is only one standard time, that of Beijing.

3   The Chinese

Language

The official spoken language in China is *putonghua*, or "common speech," otherwise known as Mandarin. It is the mother tongue of the majority and of education and media. In the many provinces where Mandarin is not the first language, people speak one of four major dialects — Cantonese, Shanghainese, Fukienese or Hakka, or a variation of these. Although most scholars believe that these four originated from the same source, they are mutually unintelligible in spoken form.

While the spoken languages vary, there is only one official *written* language; many of its characters have evolved from ancient pictographs. In the mid-1950s, the Chinese government simplified some 2,000 of the most frequently used characters (out of about 56,000) in an effort to popularize literacy and stipulated that official Chinese be written horizontally (from left to right) rather than vertically (from right to left). The government also created a standard romanized alphabetical system called *pinyin* for transliterating Chinese characters. A well-educated Chinese recognizes 6,000 to 8,000 characters, though one can get by with a working knowledge of about 1,500.

But since Mandarin is based on tones, *pinyin* is only partially helpful to the foreigner. The word *guo*, for example, can have many meanings: spoken with a high tone, it means "pot," "grasshopper" or a family name; with a rising tone, "country" or an ancient Chinese woman's scarf; with a falling-rising tone, "fruit" or "wrapping"; and with a falling tone, "passing."

Historically, Chinese has drawn from many other tongues, including Mongolian, Turkish and Japanese. English is a required subject in all universities, and in major cities, it's taught as early as elementary school. (American swear words are popular with the under-30 crowd, and businesses named Helen's Fine Cuisine and The Texas Bar are cropping up.)

Current Beijing slang includes "eating bean curd" (meaning kissing and petting) and *dageda* (for portable telephones). The latter derives from the Cantonese slang for "mob leader" — a phone-toting stock character in Hong Kong-made Kung Fu movies.

Confucianism: Still a Major Influence

Despite the Communist Party's decades-long official ban during the Cultural Revolution, Confucianism remains the principal foundation of Chinese values. (Today, Confucius' hometown of Qufu is promoted as a tourist spot.) Two thousand years ago, this great philosopher identified four basic virtues — loyalty (*zhong*), respect for parents and elders (*xiao*), benevolence (*ren*) and righteousness (*yi*) — along with five kinds of relationships:

Ruler to People. As Confucius taught, the ruler receives absolute loyalty from his people; they never question his motives or directives. In return, the ruler is wise and works only to better his people's lives.

Husband to Wife. The Confucian husband rules over his wife as a lord rules his people. She is obedient and faithful and provides her husband with sons. The husband is responsible to provide for all his wife's physical needs.

Parent to Child. Children must be loyal to their parents' wishes, giving priority to the father's, without question. The parents are obligated to raise and educate their children; children must in turn care for their parents in old age, and always show them love and respect.

Older to Younger. The Chinese have great respect for age, tending to link it with wisdom. Grandparents often rule a family; at the very least, they receive deferential treatment from children as well as grandchildren.

Friend to Friend. This is the only relationship between equals in Confucianism. Friends must be loyal and willing to help each other at every opportunity. Dishonesty between friends is a crime and demands punishment.

Self versus Group

China is a collective culture; individual Chinese are hesitant, sometimes even embarrassed to take credit for achievement. Business and political decisions are the result of consensus and virtually always represent group interests.

In the Chinese language, the word "self" carries negative connotations not unlike the Western words *selfish* and *self-centered*. This view is reflected in the etiquette of Chinese business letters, which instead of a signature bear a seal, usually a red circular stamp, of the company or government agency.

Age = Wisdom

Even though equality is one of the ultimate goals of Chinese communism, China is far from an egalitarian society. Rather, it reflects the Confucian ideal in which "sons should obey the father and subordinates obey the superior." All business activities are conducted in a manner that ensures maintenance of, and respect for, proper relations between individuals. For many Westerners, this has the appearance of an artificial class system; for the Chinese, it is the natural order of things.

Age and position are seen as sure signs of wisdom and rich experience. An old proverb counsels that "aged ginger tastes best." Young people, or those with junior positions in a company, almost unfailingly listen to and carry out the wishes of their seniors. By doing so, they not only avoid making potentially dangerous mistakes but also earn a reputation for obedience that will eventually pave their way to seniority.

As a result, older foreign businesspeople have an advantage over, and generally receive more attention than, their younger colleagues. Whatever your age, always show respect for the opinions and suggestions of your Chinese counterparts who are senior in age and position. Such an attitude will be viewed by Chinese both as a gesture of respect and as a sign of sincerity.

Saving, Losing and Giving Face

Face (*mianzi*) is the principal measure of an individual's reputation and dignity. Chinese go to great lengths to save face, while at the same time attempting to give face to others. While most Westerners appreciate this notion intellectually, they fail to understand its importance throughout Asia.

Preserving one's reputation and contributing to the reputation and prestige of others is one of the most important moral responsibilities of every Chinese.

For example, a negative response (no matter how innocent) to a friendly invitation to dinner will embarrass your Chinese host. To save his face, as well as yours, first offer a profuse apology for not being able to accept such an honor, and then propose an alternative.

If you cause someone to lose face, you can be certain you've lost the offended individual as an ally. More likely, you've lost the chance to do business with his organization and perhaps others in his industry.

Praising an associate to his superiors for his excellent contribution to the success of the group is one way of giving face. Accepting an invitation because it will show respect for the host is another. Anything you do to enhance another's reputation will eventually come back to you as an advantage.

Privacy: An Alien Concept

One immediate result of collectivism and high population density is the absence of privacy, a concept alien to Chinese. Two or three generations often live under the same roof, and many households, separated only by a common wall, share a bathroom and kitchen. As a result, talking about and commenting on the domestic matters of others is so natural that there is not even a word for privacy in Chinese.

Expect questions about your age, marital status, salary, and the price of personal items. Although your answers need not be detailed, trying to avoid answering will only invite suspicion and misunderstanding. Even in large cities such as Beijing, Shanghai and

Guangzhou, where the population is more cosmopolitan, you will still be asked intrusive questions. For the Chinese, the specifics of your answers are not as important as your willingness to respond. The main purpose of such questioning is to help build a basis for relationship. If you ask similar questions in return, you'll be seen as someone who is interested in establishing a friendship.

How the Chinese View Themselves

The Chinese take pride in their ancient philosophical and moral systems. Based on these, they see themselves as a duty-oriented people who must fulfill responsibilities to their family, community, work group, society and country. This means that business decisions and practices are more closely tied to relationships and protocol than they are in the West.

Chinese humanism focuses on the contribution of the individual to social harmony. Consequently, the Chinese appreciate the ability to maintain an outward appearance of calm and unity, even when the actual situation may have neither.

Foreign Devils

With virtually no opportunity for international exchange and communication, most of today's Chinese have grown up with a single cultural frame. Even with the rapid social changes of recent years, awareness and sensitivity toward foreigners remains largely a function of education and geography. Rural Chinese usually lack contact with the world outside their villages, whereas urban, educated Chinese are far more likely to make allowances for cultural differences.

Waiguoren, the most common term for foreigners, translates simply as "outside country person."

Other popular colloquialisms, especially for Westerners, include *yangguizi* (in the north) and *guilao* (in the south); both mean "foreign devils." These expressions are more thoughtless than pejorative, but they reflect a bitterness and distrust for colonial powers that dates back to the 19th century.

For *guilao*, even mastering China's language and customs does not guarantee acceptance. Not having been born into the Chinese "family," they are always considered different, regarded with a mixture of fear and fascination.

Americans are seen as having material wealth and enviable technology, but questionable morals and little in the way of culture (due to their short, 200-year history). Europe is admired as the center of Western civilization, despite a history that falls far short of China's 5,000-year continuum. The Japanese invasion and occupation of China before and during World War II still invokes strong feelings of hostility. And having provided economic, political and educational support to numerous small African nations in the 1960s and '70s, many Chinese view these countries as inferior.

Beliefs about Westerners

Along with national stereotypes, the Chinese harbor a number of other broadbrush beliefs about Westerners:

- They lack the knowledge that comes from hardship.
- They're straightforward, candid and seldom subtle.
- They're creative but often self-centered, and they don't recognize the importance of teamwork.
- They're passionate when it comes to personal achievement, but often impatient.

- They may respect Chinese culture but do not understand it.
- They're friendly but lack sincerity.

Chinese don't expect Westerners to know much about Chinese culture, language or history. If Westerners doing business overseas demonstrate even a little knowledge in these areas, they will quickly gain respect from their Chinese associates.

Chinese also believe that Westerners are incapable of understanding the finer points of Chinese etiquette. Consequently, they do not expect them to behave properly in certain social situations.

 ## Cultural Stereotypes

Your perceptions of China and the Chinese may be based on personal experience, on knowledge gained from others or on stereotypes. These perceptions are almost certain to color your social and business relationships.

Those based on personal experience or valid research will probably help you. Outdated or inaccurate information will create barriers. While stereotypes about China and its inhabitants vary, some are common:

A Communist Country

China is a hard-line dictatorship and the people live in poverty.

While China's system has obvious roots in Russian communism, China's government claims that their system is uniquely socialist. As previously noted, strong historical and cultural streams have mixed with communist philosophy to form the Chinese world view. For example, although the government supports the notion of a classless society, the Confucian system of hierarchies has survived into the present almost unchanged. While decisions are ascribed to many, they are often made by a select few.

Whatever the system is called, the average Chinese is more interested in harmony than in democracy and freedom. The perpetual political upheavals of the last half-century (in particular, the ten-year-long Cultural Revolution) have resulted in an almost universal yearning for peace and stability.

Worker Bees

The Chinese dedicate their lives to work and have little interest in leisure.

China's industrialization is still primitive in most areas, and because its population density is high, the only way to survive is through hard work. *"Renqin dibulan"* ("where the tiller is tireless, the land is fertile") is a popular saying. *Qin* (diligence) is a Confucian virtue and one of the most admired human qualities in China.

Because of the increasingly intense competition brought along by the market-oriented economy, hard work is further rewarded by financial prosperity. As the former premier Deng Xiaoping said, "To be rich is glorious." In response, the younger generation has set its sights on working for joint ventures or solely foreign-owned companies where longer hours are rewarded by significantly higher income and better benefits.

Since implementation of the two-day weekend, the concept of leisure has gradually taken root. Domestic tourism (not so long ago, the exclusive province of the rich) is flourishing. Special cruises along the coast line or the Yangtze River, vacation packages at popular resorts and even tours abroad are becoming increasingly fashionable and affordable.

Not Creative

The Chinese haven't invented anything since gunpowder. They can figure out the most complex scientific puzzles, but they never originate new technologies.

It's worth mentioning that along with gunpowder (which was originally used for fireworks, rather than warfare), China has given the world an extraordinary array of gifts — including paper, silk (the technique of making thread from cocoons was their exclusive secret for 3,000 years), the first printed book (long before Gutenberg), cast iron (1,800 years before Europe figured out the process), acupuncture and smallpox inoculation, the seismograph (for detecting earthquakes), porcelain ("china"), the armillary sphere (by 350 B.C., Chinese were predicting eclipses and comets and had charted 284 constellations) and a variety of marvelous foods, including the humble noodle (introduced to Italy by Marco Polo and his uncles). It has also had a rich, 4,000-year literary history and been the birthplace of Confucianism and Taoism.

That having been said, China is a society that focuses on and rewards group efforts, rather than individual ones. The Confucian "ruler-subject" tradition still informs society. This emphasis tends to favor manufacturing and service industries over research and development.

The problem has as much to do with organization as ideas. Companies of the old school are unfamiliar with decentralization. By and large, constructive criticism by employees is considered inappropriate. However, due to the pressure of marketplace competition, conservatism is slowly giving way to innovation. And a new generation of Western-educated Chinese are returning home with MBAs and modern management ideas.

Kowtowing

The Chinese obey tradition and authority without question.

Although obedience is integral to Confucianism, the relationship between subordinates and superiors is changing. The younger generation, some of whom are Western educated, are entering management positions. As a result, the tradition of blind obedience is being widely challenged.

However, the Communist Party remains omnipotent and represses those who voice dissenting opinions. For this reason, at least some of your Chinese associates will reserve their candid opinions for private conversation only.

Inscrutable

The Chinese, like other Asians, are expressionless, unemotional and almost impossible to "read".

Generally speaking, displaying one's emotions publicly is considered undignified. Since Chinese culture has traditionally valued men more than women, men, especially, feel a need to maintain a serious demeanor and refrain from exposing emotions outside of the family. This doesn't mean, however, that the Chinese do not have strong feelings. They are simply taught from an early age to mask them.

One Family, One Child

Birth control is compulsory; couples with more than one child are severely punished.

In 1956, with the population at about 500 million, Mao Zedong decided that China's strength could only grow as the number of people increased. By the late 1970s, this policy had resulted in one-fifth of the world's population and the very real possibility of starvation for many. It was then that the government instituted the One Child Policy. It has been comparatively successful in the cities; however, 70 percent of the population lives in the country. According to surveys conducted by the H. J. Heinz Company, which operates a baby food factory in Guangzhou, China's population control has resulted in cities filled with children who are doted on by their parents in ways that previous generations could not have imagined. The next few decades should indicate whether family structure can be dictated by policy.

Herbs and Aphrodisiacs

Chinese men are obsessed with sexual performance.

Confucius emphasized the importance of male fertility; Chinese males have interpreted this as an injunction to make virility the literal measure of a man. Under the ancient principle of "like imitates like," they ingest powdered rhinoceros horn, sliced and boiled stag penises, the gall bladders cut from living snakes, ginseng (a root that resembles the figure of a man) and sea slugs (which swell and enlarge when touched). Zhuang tribesmen in Guangxi Province swear by the sexual inspiration that results from eating the local turtle stew.

Few Chinese doubt the tales of leaders (both ancient and contemporary) who are constantly supplied with young (preferably virginal) maidens, whose natural fecundity is believed to feed both their lovers' power and longevity.

Regional Differences

Northern versus Southern

An old Chinese proverb says, "Mountains and waters are reflected in their people." The differences in landscape between northern and southern China distinguish their inhabitants from each other. Like their magnificent mountains and plateaus, northerners are more forthright and unrestrained. Southerners tend to be more sagacious and detail oriented, just like their exquisite southern hills and clear waters.

The differences are further enhanced by the country's culture and history. Northern Beijing has been the capital city for five dynasties lasting more than seven hundred years. As a result, northerners are feudal and political in their outlook.

Southern Shanghai, which relies on its port for business, has been the most well-developed area in the entire country in terms of industry, trade and commerce. As a result, non-Chinese have found it is easier to get southerners to understand standard international business practices than northerners. However, reaching agreement with people in the north takes less effort.

Inland Versus Coastal Areas

Historically, the coastal cities have long been exposed to foreign trade. In the 1970s, Shenzhen, a southern city close to Guangzhou (Canton) and Hong Kong, was the first city allowed to accept foreign investments. The venture's success resulted in other coastal cities being opened, and it is likely that the coastal areas will continue to be richer than inland areas. This financial difference has affected both life-styles and attitudes. People from the interior sometimes accuse coastal residents of being materialistic and snobbish, while coastal people think that those in the interior are slow to adapt to change — and probably jealous.

Culinary Regions

Despite a vast array of local cuisines, most cookbooks divide China into four gastronomic regions — Guangdong (Cantonese), Huaiyang (Shanghai), Sichuan and Shandong (Beijing).

Guangdong food is fresh and light; ingredients are cooked quickly in their own juices. Huaiyang is sweeter and rich in seasonings (rice wine, ginger, green onion, sesame oil and others). Sichuan ("red earth," after the region's maroon soil) features tangy spices and peppers. Shandong features wheat buns and pancakes rather than rice.

Other food types include Mongol (*steak tartare* dates back to the era of Genghis Khan), Manchu (lamb stews and beef barbecues), Xinjiang (goat and camel cheese, meat and vegetable kebabs cooked on charcoal) and Tibetan (lots of barley and yak butter).

For more on Chinese food, see Chapter 20.

6 Government & Business

Good Cats Catch Rats

In keeping with its socialist philosophy, the Chinese government controls the business sector. And though it claims to have replaced its traditional, planned economy with a market-driven one, the government supervises every aspect of this sector, too.

Still, their approach is a pragmatic one. Credit is provided to industries that generate more exports, technology is subsidized, developing industries are protected with lower tariffs and private industry (slowly replacing state-owned enterprises) is encouraged.

The government explains these policies as part of an emerging, Chinese-style socialism. Perhaps Deng Xiaoping's political proverb puts it best: "It doesn't matter if a cat is black or white, as long as it catches rats." The role of China's government in the country's economic development will remain strong for the foreseeable future.

Perpetual Uncertainty

One of the most frustrating aspects of investing in China for non-Chinese is that the government never discusses new business policies and regulations with foreigners, nor announces such changes in advance. (For example, they recently withdrew the tax-free benefits given to foreign joint ventures' imported equipment and added on heavy duties.)

The most effective way to deal with such challenges is to have your local Chinese partner or consultant work continually on obtaining government clearances or approvals of your project, while maintaining close relationships with local officials at different levels.

Perseverance has its rewards. Three major success stories:

- Proctor & Gamble has cornered China's shampoo market with Head & Shoulders (a dandruff product), despite the fact that it costs three times as much as some local brands.

- Pepsi Cola has twelve factories in China, another nine under construction, and a total investment of $500 million.

- Volkswagens can be seen negotiating Shanghai's traffic both as private vehicles and as taxi cabs.

Lone Dragons

Traditionally, most Chinese enterprises were large, state-owned plants and factories infamous for their inefficiency. And until recently, their profits and losses were absorbed by the government, thereby creating no incentive for the managers to become better organized.

But in recent years, the government has been promoting entrepreneurship. Two types of entrepreneurs have emerged. The first are managers of state-owned enterprises who have been given fuller control over daily operations and responsibility for profits and losses. Depending on their success, these companies will eventually either close or be sold to private entrepreneurs (in China or abroad).

The second type of entrepreneur comes from the private sector. There are now well over twenty million registered private and individual businesses in China, ranging from hole-in-the-wall shops to multi-million-dollar feed-processing plants. And the number is growing every day.

This phenomenon is especially significant for foreign businesspeople, as it provides a basis for dialogue and negotiation. However, it's important to note that Chinese entrepreneurs — like *tai-pans* of older, more traditional businesses — tend to take a dynastic approach, keeping ownership and management in the same hands. The downside of this approach is that such companies don't always survive when their stewardships are passed down. ("Wealth never survives the third generation" warns an old Chinese proverb.)

Building up a core of professional (non-family) managers who play a vital role in a company's decision-making processes is still considered "un-Asian."

Outsiders Welcome... Sometimes

As part of its preparation for joining the World Trade Organization in 1992, the Chinese either abolished or reduced tariffs (an average of 7.3 percent) on a total of 3,596 import categories. And effective April 1, 1996, they reduced them an additional 23 percent in an effort to promote free trade and foreign investment.

China has also established Special Zones for Economic and Technology Development (SZETD) in 32 cities. In them, foreign investors pay a 15 percent business tax rate, compared to 24 percent and 33 percent tax rates elsewhere in the country. The government has specifically expressed desire for foreign capital for railroads, highways, power plants and telecommunications — all formerly protected "national industries."

However, foreign companies will still find it difficult to compete with local manufacturers, especially makers of consumer appliances. Market share can only be traded for advanced high technology. Import licenses are still required for sugar, fertilizer, grain, wine, tobacco, wool, steel, computers, timber and wood pulp. The Ministry of Foreign Trade and Economic Cooperation (MOFTEC) publishes annual lists of items restricted for import. Quotas are established for investments and, once they are met, no further investments are allowed for that year.

Politics and Business = Bedfellows

Politics and business go hand in hand. A company's activities are greatly influenced (even controlled) by its political identity. A company owned by a government ministry will certainly be more successful and stable than one owned privately. In fact, government-owned companies openly advertise their relationship, as it projects a sense of reliability and financial stability. All enterprises try to enhance themselves by posting congratulatory messages from government officials, publicizing ribbon-cuttings by prominent leaders, or having photographs taken with high-level bureaucrats.

On the other side of this equation, Chinese government officials are eager to demonstrate their support for economic development any way they can. They understand that the best way to maintain power is to satisfy consumer demands and encourage foreign investment. As a non-Chinese conducting business in China, it's to your advantage to make friends with the Commission for Foreign Economic Relations & Trade, the Planning Commission, the Tax Bureau and the Administration of Industry & Commerce.

Networking, Chinese-style

The business structure in China consists of invisible social networks. Members of these networks enjoy many advantages when it comes to licensing, permits, compliance, market access, loans and the issuing of passports and visas. In response, foreign and joint venture companies work to maintain good relationships with current government officials and to hire former ones as consultants.

An increasing number of bureaucrats are leaving their government positions for private business and its enormous potential for financial gain. Lack of appropriate regulations allows them to freely manipulate their government connections on behalf of their new employer.

In addition, many relatives of high-ranking Communist Party officials now hold senior management positions in prominent companies, posing substantial political, social and business challenges to those without such insider connections.

Although Party bureaucrats don't officially admit to the existence of government corruption, their recent and much-publicized campaign against just such corruption resulted in a number of arrests of persons with family connections in the politburo. The penalties included a death sentence for a provincial governor's spouse found guilty of embezzlement.

7 The Work Environment

Danwei: An Extension of Family

In times of hardship, war or social chaos, the Chinese family has always served as a bastion against the outside world. Even during peace and prosperity, business and social connections are first made with family members, and only then with family friends. This practice was eventually extended to include the *danwei* (work unit) to which every worker must belong. A Chinese who cannot be identified by family and *danwei* has no identity — and therefore no strength or protection.

In addition to a job, the *danwei* provides — or denies — housing, health insurance, child care, pension, and in many cases, facilities where employees and their family can eat, bathe and obtain childcare. The *danwei* also controls its members' professional lives by maintaining dossiers that include information on family background, political activities and job performance. Without permission from his *danwei* to transfer his dossier, it's virtually impossible for a worker to join another unit.

In many ways, the *danwei* is like a traditional Confucian family, with the supervisor acting as a father who commands the loyalty and respect of his wife and children, in return for which he looks after their basic needs. Although China has been strongly influenced by Western economic reforms in recent years, most Chinese still believe that being a model family member and *danwei* worker is the most responsible (and safest) course of action.

Iron Rice Bowl versus Porcelain Rice Bowl

The *danwei* system is commonly known as the "iron rice bowl" where people "eat from one big pot." The unbreakable bowl symbolizes guaranteed lifetime employment, protection from demotion, and a virtual lack of salary differentials on either a skills or performance basis. The only causes for dismissal are criminal activity or flagrant absenteeism without a medical excuse — either of which brings disgrace to the *danwei*, the employee and his family.

Jobs for university graduates are guaranteed, but they are assigned by government employment agencies that pay little or no attention to a worker's personal goals or interests. The government has recently begun to dismantle this largely inefficient system, exchanging the iron rice bowl for a porcelain one, that is, a more flexible approach to hiring and firing based on performance and skill levels.

An increasing number of people, university students in particular, now seek out positions with joint venture enterprises by attending "talent" or job fairs or by applying in person during their last year of school. Advertising is gradually becoming an accepted means of matching potential employees with positions. Although salaries in most newly established enterprises are considerably higher than for those who still hold iron rice bowl jobs, job security is not guaranteed.

The government has set a national goal of implementing the contract-labor system in all enterprises by the beginning of the 21st century. But as the old job assignment system has not been abolished completely, private enterprises are finding that hiring workers away from their *danwei* is problematic. Workers must obtain both transfer approvals and residence permits (without which they cannot move to another part of the country and for which the *danwei* often charges large release fees). And to effectively compete for the best talent, foreign-owned and joint venture businesses must provide benefit packages that include housing, healthcare, childcare and a retirement fund.

So, while the government officially supports the notion of increased job mobility, it also maintains regulations that discourage the possibility.

Economic Boom — Rising Unemployment

Despite a steady economic growth rate (lately, among the highest in the world), China is experiencing high unemployment and underemployment. There are two reasons: the financial collapse of many state-owned enterprises and the aforementioned transition from assigned, life-long employment to a contract-labor system. There are now more than 200 million workers in the cities. Although the official unemployment rate hovered around 2.5 percent in the early 1990s, off-the-record estimates by officials put the urban unemployment rate two to four times higher — which means that there are anywhere from 10 to 20 million unemployed in the cities alone.

In addition, shrinking rural employment opportunities have driven as many as 100 million — the "floating" population — to the cities. While many Chinese policy makers support the expansion of the private business sector as a way to reduce unemployment, others are concerned that a more efficient private sector could put even more people out of work. Meanwhile, the government continues to prop up inefficient and oversized state enterprises.

Straddling Two Boats

Loyalty to one employer is almost nonexistent, as many urban workers maintain a second (or even third) job in order to survive. This is known as "straddling two boats"; if one boat sinks, the other will still be floating. In Beijing and Guangzhou, for example, almost one third of state workers have second jobs. In Shanghai and Chongqing, the proportion is estimated at 40 percent.

Soaring Literacy

Education is highly respected in Chinese society, largely because of the Confucian notion that "he who excels in learning can be an official." Although hampered by severe financial problems and endless political movements during the first fifty years of communist rule, China's literacy rate has soared from 20 percent to more than 80 percent.

Veterans of the Communist Revolution who, up until now, have held important positions at every level of the country's social system, are gradually being replaced by much younger and better-educated professionals.

Long Negotiations

Decision making in China is based on gathering consensus. Major decisions are made by the leader of the collective within the system only after a wide range of reviews and discussions by all persons concerned.

This approach has major implications for foreign businesspeople. One is that negotiations will usually take much longer than Westerners (in particular) think necessary. Expect many meetings with frequent recesses, during which the Chinese confer with their colleagues and superiors outside the meeting room. The advantage to this approach is that once decisions are made, they tend to be sound and easily executed, as all the implications and possible ramifications have been carefully considered.

Pitfalls of Bureaucracy

Bureaucratic meddling by party and government officials is a major problem in northern and inland areas. Local party secretaries, municipal managers, tax officers and the like can make establishing and running a business very difficult, especially for foreigners. A tax may be imposed on a company simply because the local coffers are low, or worse, because a local official doesn't like someone in that company. Chinese bureaucrats are liable to engage in all kinds of intrigues, including the sabotage of projects for personal gain or revenge.

Having powerful officials for friends can be a major asset. Land-use rights, tax bases and many other regulations can be relaxed if the right people give their consent. This is especially true in more remote areas, where wages are lower and the need for business development is greater.

Feng Shui

In ancient times, a tradition arose that China sits atop an Earth Dragon, over which currents of wind (*feng*) and water (*shui*) flow. Chinese emperors consulted *feng shui* experts before building a palace or waging war, to determine if the structure or battle in question rested on the dragon's back (ideal), neck or head (bad) or eyeball (the worst thing possible).

Despite the "destruction of four olds" (old thinking, old culture, old tradition, old customs) during the ten-year Cultural Revolution (1966–1976), *feng shui* is still widely (if surreptitiously) practiced. Its principles are applied to the placement of highways, telephone poles, offices, and even the chopping down of trees. Buildings, even in the best positions, must be aligned to prevent bad spirits from slipping in. The strategic placement of a mirror can divert them; doors should always face south.

Some Chinese believe that the untimely demise of Bruce Lee (the Hong Kong screen idol and martial arts expert) had to do with the fact that he lived in an unlucky house.

Westerners tend to find the concept quaint. But most China-based employers will find that consulting with, and following the advice of, a *feng shui* professional will reassure both their staff and their associates.

Women in Business

Traditional Roles

For centuries, China's patriarchal society defined women as "accessories of a man." Women could be traded as commodities and a man could "own" several wives. An old Chinese proverb advises, "A woman's virtue is that she has no talent." Education for most women was limited to learning how to cook and sew. Upper-class women learned to sing, play chess, read and draw so they could better serve upper-class men. A man could divorce his spouse for being talkative, for only bearing daughters, or for being jealous (that is, for being reluctant to accept her husband's concubines). For women, however, divorce was impossible. Although in recent history, many women have made significant contributions to (and even sacrificed their lives for) social change, women were almost nonexistent in civil service and business until the 1950s.

To Be a Tigress

Nowadays, "Women hold up half of the sky," as Mao Zedong declared. Officially, a woman has the right to expect pay and status equal to that of a man holding the same job. It is becoming more common for women to hold executive positions in factories, companies and government offices.

Still, equality remains an uphill battle. "Tigress" is a widely used derogatory term for women who stand up for their principles. Confucian male attitudes still linger in business environments, and it's not unusual to see women play a purely decorative role in a company. Even women who have senior positions encounter resistance to their leadership.

However, most Chinese businessmen recognize that Western women hold positions at the highest levels of business and government and try, therefore, to adjust their expectations of, and behavior toward, foreign women.

Strategies for Western Businesswomen

Foreign businesswomen coming to China are not likely to encounter overt discrimination. They may, in fact, be much admired and respected because Chinese (especially Chinese women) will assume that they must be persons of exceptional competence to be given an overseas assignment.

There are some things that Western businesswomen can do to make their trip more successful. Negative comments or criticism on any aspect of women's rights in China must be avoided. Public discussion of anyone's sexual orientation will draw unwelcome attention and unnecessary trouble. Always, of course, show equal respect and professionalism to both Chinese men and women.

Before sending a female representative to China, the home company should prepare her and her delegates thoroughly. An introduction letter that clearly indicates the female leader's position, her credentials and accomplishments should be sent to China in advance. Her business card should have an authoritative title (especially in Chinese translation) to emphasize her decision-making power.

At meetings, the female representative should always be introduced first to the seniors of the Chinese team. She should then introduce her colleagues to the Chinese. Team members should avoid disagreement with her in the presence of Chinese associates. The female delegation leader should always be the first to respond to any questions and requests. Only then, if appropriate and needed, should she direct the issue to one of her colleagues. By displaying self-confidence and poise, a foreign businesswoman may, in fact, be able to accomplish things much faster than a male counterpart.

Foreign businesswomen are usually invited to business banquets, sight-seeing trips, or evening entertainment. If she's unable to attend, she should formally designate a member of her team to represent her.

9 Making Connections

The Chinese do not like to do business with strangers. They negotiate relationships rather than contracts. Attempts to establish solid connections often fail because foreigners simply don't pay enough attention to cultivating personal foundations.

You Gotta Have Guanxi

Guanxi (literally, "relationships") is best translated into English as "connections." Using one's *guanxi* to get things done which are impossible otherwise is commonly known as *zouhoumen* (going through the back door).

Obtaining official approval for a joint venture in China takes from six to eighteen months. However, if you have cultivated relationships with the government bureaucrats involved in the approval process, the process will probably take much less time. Connections made through family or clans (those from the same geographical area or who speak the same dialect) tend to be particularly fruitful.

In today's business environment in China, executives and entrepreneurs work constantly to maintain and expand their network of connections.

Networks can extend to other companies and individuals in Hong Kong, Taiwan, Southeast Asia, and even to Europe and the U.S. While the purpose of such contacts is often mutual financial benefit, the criteria are the same as for personal connections: trustworthiness and loyalty.

The Tea Gets Cold...

Developing strong *guanxi* takes an enormous amount of patience and persistence. The Chinese dislike casual relationships. "The tea gets cold once the guest leaves," they say. To keep the tea warm, it's essential to maintain ongoing friendly contacts both in business and social situations.

Chinese identify three phases in the process of getting to know somebody: know their name, know their face (appearance), then know their heart (true self). It always helps if your name has been referred to them by someone they already know. Don't expect a Chinese to trust you simply because you've shown up. The process of getting to know your heart takes more time.

The effort required to cultivate a relationship will not be a waste of time. Frequent visits and calls to your business connections will provide you with the opportunity to evaluate their character and intentions. This knowledge can be crucial when it comes to deciding how far you should take the business relationship.

Intermediaries

The most effective way to develop your connections is to involve a Chinese intermediary from your own country in the process. The Chinese go-between should be someone who can introduce you to reliable connections in China, and who is culturally sensitive to the business etiquette of both countries. Such an intermediary will help you to:

- be more quickly accepted, so that you can start building your *guanxi* more effectively
- obtain more thorough and accurate information about your potential business associates and their intentions
- avoid making mistakes in local customs

Going through an intermediary will also increase the comfort level of your Chinese associates, who are relative newcomers to the modern international business arena.

Written Introductions

If you have friends who have connections in China, ask them to write a letter introducing you and your company, explaining the reasons for your visit and providing an itinerary. As a next step, you should write to request an appointment. If you do get a meeting, bring an additional letter of introduction from your friend that affirms your character and trustworthiness.

If you don't have indirect connections to China, contact your government's consulates in the cities you plan to visit and request a list of appropriate businesses to contact. When you arrive, try to meet the consul who has helped you and ask him to introduce you to businesses before you actually visit them. Social standing is very important in China. An introduction from an official of your government will create a good first impression.

The Importance of Business Cards

Exchanging cards is a basic part of doing business. Your card should be printed in both English and Chinese. (Practice the Chinese pronunciation of your company's name well in advance.) Consult a native mainland Chinese for a good translation.

When you present your card, be sure that the side with the Chinese translation faces up toward the recipient. Hold the upper corners of the card with the thumbs and forefingers of both hands. Receive your Chinese associate's card with both hands, read it carefully and then be sure to put it away. Leaving someone's business card behind is considered rude.

A Few Tips about Telephones

About twelve years ago, few people in China had telephones. Business was done in person, by messenger, or by telegram. Today, Beijing and Shanghai phone numbers have ten digits (up from only five as a result of the demand). Fax machines, pagers and cellular phones are in evidence, and e-mail and Internet connections are being introduced.

It's difficult for foreign visitors to find public telephones. Many are tucked away in small, family-run shops (if it's sitting on the counter, it's probably for public use), and non-standard signs, sometimes handwritten on paper board, are usually in Chinese.

Pay phones are always available in hotels and post offices. Be sure to check the access code for an outside line before dialing from your hotel room, as they vary greatly from place to place.

10 Strategies for Success

The Chinese proverb *"Ru xiang sui su"* (literally, "Enter place, follow custom") carries the same meaning as the English saying, "When in Rome, do as the Romans do." No matter how illogical or inefficient Chinese ways seem, you still need to learn them. Here are some guidelines.

1. **Understand the business-development process and build your network around it.**

In China, direct solicitation is unnecessary. Instead, concentrate on establishing a network with the appropriate institutions. If you are setting up a joint venture, it is important to not only become well acquainted with the local factory managers, but also to establish personal relationships with the local government officials who will be involved in your business plan.

2. **Be patient with temporary rules.**

In addition to an increasing number of new laws that govern foreign businesses in China, there are many temporary (and confusing) regulations. Failure to follow them can have serious consequences; consider hiring an international business law firm that has continuing involvement in China. Such a firm will have current information as well as model legal documents in which much of the wording is approved by the Ministry of Foreign Trade and Economic Cooperation (MOFTEC), the highest authority for foreign investment approval.

3.   Take your time.

China's enormous bureaucracy and its ever-changing legal and economic landscapes guarantee that nothing gets done quickly. In addition, Chinese culture teaches that one should be suspicious of too much haste and should proceed cautiously as a matter of principle.

4.   Listen more, talk less.

Saying something that later proves to be wrong will damage your credibility with Chinese associates. "A single word is worth a thousand pieces of gold." Therefore, the accuracy and thoughtfulness of what you say is much more important than how quickly you respond. Being a good listener is considered a virtue.

5.   Be modest and respectful.

Chinese consider boasting or self-promotion to be very poor form and will usually minimize their own accomplishments. In contrast, a knowledgeable, capable person with a modest and respectful attitude enjoys great admiration and respect.

11

Time

An Aversion to Deadlines

Written Chinese does not have tenses. There are, however, words to indicate the passage of time — tomorrow, now, and so forth. The Western concept that "time is money" is widely known among Chinese involved in international business, but they generally resist being constrained by deadlines.

For the Chinese, time is fluid, rather than something that is best compartmentalized into minutes, days, weeks, months and years. This applies to both their social and business lives. While Westerners pride themselves on guaranteeing delivery dates, with product quality sometimes suffering in the process, the Chinese take a different approach. They prefer to elicit consensus that a product is fully functional, wait for an auspicious moment, and then unveil a thoroughly tested prototype.

Appointments

Before telephone service became more widely available about a decade ago, the idea of an appointment was not practical, and time and energy wasted by one party's unavailability was usual. Now, however, Chinese businesspeople are beginning to realize that appointments are not only a matter of convenience, but also of respect.

There is a stark difference between the pace of government offices and private businesses. Bureaucrats and minor officials like to keep customers waiting as a matter of face (it increases their sense of importance). Low efficiency costs the state, but workers have little to lose. However, in retail businesses where salespeople receive commissions, service is swift and friendly and staff are eager to help.

Getting Things From Here To There

For every 1,000 square kilometers of land in the U.S., there are 640 km of road and 51 km of rail. In China, there are 108 km of road (their condition varies greatly) and 8 km of rail. Transportation connections between air, water, railroad and highways are poor. It's not surprising, then, that things take a long time to move from place to place. And it costs more to transport a shipping container from southern China to Hong Kong than to move it from Hong Kong to Europe or North America.

Many airports have only one or two runways and are inefficiently managed. A limited number of airplanes, combined with unexpected weather, add to the problem. Many Chinese prefer train travel, finding it more reliable and economical.

12 Business Meetings

Preparation

Business meetings with foreigners are formal occasions in China. Nevertheless, many Chinese still believe that the burden is on the foreigners, since they're the ones coming to do business. As a result, the Chinese often arrive at meetings ill-prepared. Don't be discouraged, and remember that it's crucial to have an agenda and stick to it.

Before the meeting, send a list of your team members (in order of seniority or importance), along with a brief resume of each, to the Chinese, and request a similar list from them. Include translated materials about your business as well.

Even in big cities, the availability and quality of commercial clerical support is unpredictable, so bring enough copies of all your documents. If you need audio or video equipment, it's much safer to bring your own. (Don't forget a 220v voltage converter and a standard Chinese plug.) Special requests should be made to the Chinese as early as possible, and in the absence of a definite response, assume that the request can't be met.

Scheduling

Scheduling should be done well in advance. Not only do you need the time for thorough preparation, but you should also give the Chinese sufficient time to make proper arrangements. Although you are expected to meet with people of the same level as your team, request a meeting with the senior official of the company or government ministry. The meeting may be simply symbolic, but it has important implications beyond a courtesy call — it demonstrates sincerity and respect from your side and reflects seriousness and support from the Chinese.

Last-minute delays or cancellations are not unusual, especially when senior officials are involved. To make amends, the Chinese may arrange special functions for you, such as sight-seeing or banquets. Under such circumstances, express your understanding rather than your disappointment.

Small Talk First

Dress formally and be on time. Punctuality is considered a sign of both respect and the seriousness of your intent.

On arrival, your team will be led into a conference room where your Chinese associates will probably already be waiting. Enter the room in order of rank; the Chinese always assume the first to enter is the head of the group. The head of the Chinese group is usually introduced by a subordinate, often the interpreter. Then, the Chinese leader will introduce his team. Then, you should do the same.

During handshakes and an exchange of business cards, you are expected to greet everyone by saying *ni hao* ("How do you do?") with a slight nod of your head. You will be led to one side of the (usually rectangular) table; the Chinese team will sit on the other side, seating in descending order of rank, with their leader in the middle. Hot tea is usually served.

The Chinese usually start a meeting with small talk about your trip, hotel or the weather. Follow suit; or as the Chinese say, *Ke sui zhu bian* ("The guest follows the host"). Trying to initiate business right away will make the Chinese uncomfortable.

First Day Protocol

The head of the Chinese team usually delivers a welcome statement and then lets the guest present his business. As noted before, the Chinese look to the leader for all meaningful dialogues. Therefore, the head of your group should speak directly to the head of the Chinese team, rather than to the interpreter.

The Chinese approach to business discussions is to begin in general terms and only then move toward specifics. Avoid presenting too many details before "the big picture" is understood.

Your typical presentation for the first meeting should take no more than 20 minutes. Maintain a direct, candid approach and clarify anything that seems unclear. (Questions and details can be considered in the discussion that follows.) Acknowledge the importance of your deadlines but don't push too hard on this issue; it will only serve to mislead, or possibly even annoy, the Chinese.

Concluding the Meeting

The head of the Chinese team will usually signal the end of a meeting by making a closing statement, which often sets the tone for future meetings and even the entire project. Your team leader should then express appreciation on behalf of your team and company for a good meeting and for the host's hospitality. This is also the time to emphasize your company's desire to establish a long-term, mutually beneficial, relationship. If you don't refer to the prospect of business in your closing statement, the Chinese assume a lack of interest in moving ahead.

While handshakes are more common in Hong Kong than in Shanghai, they are appropriate at the meeting's end. As a guest, you should initiate the handshake with the head of the Chinese team, and then continue with other members in descending order of rank. As a courtesy, the Chinese will let your team leave the meeting room first and then accompany you to the elevator or front gate.

Be sure to document the important points of discussion, as well as general intents or agreements, then distribute these notes to the Chinese soon after the meeting.

A Note on Responsibility

Many Chinese officials are hesitant to take responsibility for making decisions. While you may be ready, even before your business trip, to make choices and commitments based on your own best judgment, most Chinese will avoid doing so, in case their decisions turn out to be bad ones. Historically, this has been an effective tactic for self-protection in uncertain times.

The last thing you should do is push for a decision. Instead, expand your network of allies to include most of the personnel involved. Diplomatically assist your Chinese associates in reaching an agreement among themselves. Individuals are immune from blame if a decision is based on consensus.

13   Negotiating with the Chinese

Opening Protocol

The first goal in a negotiation is to reach *yixiang shu* (a letter of intent), which expresses mutual interest and a desire to cooperate. The language of these letters, which have no binding effect, is usually vague and ambiguous.

When setting up a joint venture, other documents required during the course of a negotiation will include a *lixiang shu* (project proposal), *kexingxing baogao* (feasibility studies) and a *hezi qiye hetongshu* (joint venture contract). Once these documents have been approved by the appropriate government authorities, a business license application can be filed.

East versus West

There are some very basic differences between Chinese and Western approaches to negotiation and understanding these differences is essential to success.

* **Honesty versus Deception.** Generally speaking, the Chinese believe that Westerners are friendly, honest and trusting and that they conduct business with a high level of integrity.

However, they don't feel compelled to behave in a similar fashion. Deception and the exploitation of weaknesses are time-honored strategies in China's business, military and political arenas.

- **Naivete versus Experience.** The Chinese believe that the lack of a sophisticated historical and cultural background (especially in the U.S., with its comparatively short and pleasant history) has left Westerners naive. Their own turbulent 5,000-year history, Chinese believe, has created hard-earned strength and shrewdness, and the ability to take advantage of another's weaknesses.

- **Short Term versus Long Term.** Chinese find many Westerners, especially North Americans, lack the patience to build up long-term business relationships, concentrating instead on immediate financial gain. The Chinese value long-term benefits and are willing to wait.

- **"Old-Fashioned" Practices.** Chinese society is based on commonly held ethical codes and moral principles rather than on legislation. There is no systematized code of business law, and enforcement of existing regulations is erratic. Business deals are often sealed with a handshake or the nod of a head.

- **Toeing the Party Line.** The Communist Party influences every aspect of China's social and business realms. All business terms must be compatible with official Party politics.

Sun Tzu's Art of War

Most Chinese negotiators are well versed in psychological bargaining tactics, and many of these were penned as military strategies over 2,000 years ago by the mysterious Sun Zi Bin Fa (also known as Sun Tzu). His book, *The Art of War,* is based on the premise that as wars involve death and determine the fates of nations, they must be carefully and rationally planned.

The ideal victory, Sun Tzu explained, was to subjugate without actually engaging in combat — through diplomatic coercion, thwarting enemy plans and alliances, and frustrating enemy strategy. Avoiding strong force was seen not as cowardice but wisdom; analysis and self-control were key.

The Art of War was first translated about two hundred years ago by a French missionary, and its thirteen strategies for dealing with thirteen different circumstances are believed to have influenced Napoleon Bonaparte, the Nazi High Command and even the planning of Operation Desert Storm. In 1972, during the excavation of a Han Dynasty tomb of a high-ranking official, archeologists unearthed previously unknown sections of Sun Tzu's treatise — carved on remarkably preserved bamboo slips. Subsequent translations turned this ancient work, written for military commanders and their feudal overlords in an era of chariot warfare and bronze-tipped spears, into an international best-seller. In the 1990s, *The Art of War* has found new life as a bible for top Japanese and Western executives.

Another source of negotiation tactics are the Taoist-based "thirty-six strategies," which date back about 1,500 years and were originally composed in six segments of six. (A traditional saying is, *liu liu da shun* — two sixes make a great success.) These segments (confusing opponents, gobbling up opponents, and so on) are so much a part of China's overall heritage that even children are familiar with a few of them. In the modern business world, they're seen as defenses against those who operate unfairly.

Top Ten Chinese Tactics

1. **Using friendship to gain concessions.** Friendship is important in dealing with Chinese. However, warm hospitality, banquets and entertainments may be subtle manipulations to put you in the position of a debtor, making it difficult for you to refuse a proposed agreement.

2. **Playing off competitors.** Chinese may negotiate with several competing companies at the same time, using offers from these competitors against each other.

3. **Getting the other side to show their cards first.** By requiring you to make elaborate presentations and asking many questions afterward, the Chinese are able to gain valuable information about your position, concerns and "bottom line."

4. **Using proponents to practice their own skills.** On multimillion-dollar projects, the Chinese usually conduct preliminary research to determine which company is considered best in its industry. They then carry out mock negotiations with other competitors to gain experience and knowledge.

5. **Taking advantage of foreigners' investment or fear of failure.** The Chinese are well aware that foreigners must have spent a good deal of time and money to come to China, and that they do not wish to go home empty-handed. To increase the pressure, they may appear indifferent and/ or make increasing demands for concessions.

6. **Using your own words against you.** Chinese have been known to quote a foreigner's own words, which might have been spoken under very different circumstances, to refute his current position.

7. **Flattery.** Chinese are not above heaping praise on foreigners, either for personal attributes or business acumen, in order to stroke egos and thus catch the other side off guard.

8. **Delaying negotiations until the last minute.** If they know the date of your departure, Chinese may intentionally hold up substantive negotiations until the day before you plan to leave.

9. **Inflating prices and hiding the real bottom line.** When Chinese appear to give in to your demand for lower prices, it might be because their original price was abnormally high.

10. **Using interpreters.** The Chinese will use interpreters during negotiations, even when their English is fluent.

Tips for Foreign Negotiators

- Always maintain your integrity and professionalism, and behave in a friendly manner both inside and outside the negotiating room.

- Make impressive presentations, but be sure not to discuss any sensitive technological information before reaching a full agreement.

- Take careful notes and promptly clarify any ambiguities on important points.

- Play by Chinese rules — including playing off competitors and padding the price.

- Leave room for compromise, but do not give in too quickly or dramatically.

- Show your willingness to walk away, and let the other side know that failure to agree is an acceptable alternative to a bad deal.

- Be patient and calm.

- Have an attorney review the contract in both languages before you sign it.

- Finally, approach negotiations and all business in China from the standpoint of long-term involvement. Compromising with the Chinese over a specific issue can sometimes result in enormous future benefits.

The Language Barrier

An interpreter is an important member of any business delegation. Although English is a required subject in the general curriculum of universities (and English instruction starts as early as elementary school in major cities), students are hampered by a lack of native English-speaking teachers.

Usually, a member of the Chinese delegation will act as their interpreter. But under no circumstances should you depend on him. Although there is little chance that he will intentionally try to mislead you, it's very likely that he will be more skilled at translating English to Mandarin than Mandarin to English.

Tips on Using Interpreters

- Find an interpreter who is bicultural and bilingual, and thus able to distinguish the nuances of both cultures and the inflections of both languages.
- Spend as much time as possible getting acquainted with your interpreter before the negotiations begin.
- Explain the significance of the negotiations to the interpreter and let him understand your position on issues in advance. Make sure that he has at least a general understanding of the technical terms in both languages.
- Try to speak in short sentences. Avoid using any words and expressions that are vague or

subject to misinterpretation. Pause after every few sentences to allow for translation.

Unless you understand Chinese, you will have no way of knowing if your points have been accurately translated and fully understood. Therefore, you should repeat your important points at different times, stating them in different words or from different perspectives. And be aware that negotiations involving translation take two or three times longer than meetings conducted in a consensual language.

Contracts, Chinese Style

Because of a lack of institutionalized business law, many Chinese officials and business people, especially in remote areas, have little or no regard for written contracts. However, in those areas with a heavy concentration of foreign investment, the concept of contracts as legally binding documents has been widely accepted.

The Chinese prefer short agreements stating principles, with the details being worked out by subordinates at a later date. Avoid this kind of situation if you can. It increases the chance of misunderstanding on both sides and necessitates further negotiations, which will undoubtedly be time-consuming and costly.

 ## Business Outside the Law

The Black Market

Until recently, the government's vice grip on the economy left little room for maneuvering for personal financial gain outside of official channels. However, with unemployment increasing and the inflation rate soaring, the government has been "overlooking" the fact that many people are holding second (or even third) jobs without paying the appropriate taxes.

Illegal street currency dealers are not uncommon (they like U.S. dollars best). They're very efficient, and a lot faster, than the often rude and apathetic staff of official bank exchanges. They also trade in counterfeit bills.

Beware. Now and then, the local police conduct a dragnet, and along with the street vendors, they may scoop up a tourist or two. The vendors face severe fines and jail sentences; the tourists are set free with a stern warning. But if you're in China on business and the authorities are so inclined, you may suddenly find yourself being known as a currency speculator.

Pirates' Paradise

The piracy of international patents and intellectual property in China is rampant, particularly in the designer clothing, computer software and laser disk industries. While there's no hard evidence that these violations are sanctioned, many of the businesses making huge profits on these goods are legitimate companies with licenses and approvals from government agencies.

What most non-Chinese may be unaware of, however, is that pirates are also sabotaging *Chinese* trademark credibility. In the past, China criticized Western demands for copyright protection as bullying and interference. But increasingly, demands for protection and compensation are coming from local talent.

China's leading rock star, Cui Jian, would probably top international lists for total record sales, if only there was a way to verify the numbers. His manager estimates that fans have purchased at least ten times the 1.2 million CDs and tapes on which Cui Jian collects royalties. (China has the largest pirate music market in the world. Most of the goods end up in eastern Europe, the EU and Russia.) The company that invented and markets the first Chinese-language word-processing program sold in China estimates that one real program sells for every ten "knock-offs." A best-selling Chinese novelist who specializes in writing about pimps and prostitutes is frustrated that imitations of his work are being churned out in his name. Despite an exclusive license from the Ministry of Health, scientist Wu Cheng discovered that at least half a dozen factories were manufacturing his formula for a heart medicine made from fermented earthworms.

In 1995, the government passed a law allowing consumers to return fake products for full refunds.

Still, little has changed. Organizations set up to protect Chinese interests have pirates as members. Plants and factories that have been forced to close (often due to pressure from the United States) magically reopen, or simply move their warehouses. In the end, even flagrant piracy is very difficult to prove.

Graft at All Levels

In the more affluent South (notably in Guangdong Province), corruption is particularly prevalent, since opportunities for illegal payments are more readily available. Officials have been known to use inside information (along with public or company funds) to manipulate incipient Chinese stock exchanges. The government bond market created in 1991 all but collapsed within one year because of rampant speculation by inept traders.

In the mid-1990s, the government announced the arrest of 100 of its own employees in Sichuan Province for operating an illegal stock exchange. A recent political scandal was the dismissal of Chen Xitong, a member of the Politburo of the Communist Party (the most powerful core of China's ruling party leadership) for accepting kickbacks from Hong Kong development interests.

And it is not uncommon for aid monies (collected to benefit flood victims, for example) to be squandered on bureaucratic banquets.

An Evolving Legal System

China has voluminous regulations, but interpretation and enforcement are arbitrary and often depend on the point that the authorities are trying to make at any given time. Traditionally, China has regulated its affairs by a combination of central decrees and local official discretion, rather than by legislation and enforcement. Regulations are either too vague or overly specific, and sometimes even contradictory.

Moreover, China still lacks solid business, commercial and securities laws, not to mention accounting standards. Civil laws are rudimentary and criminal laws are draconian. Although the Chinese leadership has stated that it intends to reform the legal system and allow greater autonomy for attorneys and the judiciary, most lawyers continue to be government employees rather than independent advocates.

Recent dramatic changes in China have brought into conflict the traditional desire for order and the Western-influenced desire for freedom from control. The next few years should see an increase in this tension, along with the establishment of a more effective commercial and legal framework within which business can be conducted with greater confidence.

Names & Greetings

The order of Chinese names is family name first, then given name. Thus, Zhang Wenqiang should be addressed as Mr. Zhang. Among some 440 family names, the 100 most common ones account for 90 percent of the total population. Brides in China do not adopt their husband's surnames.

Among Chinese, a popular way to address each other, regardless of gender, is to add an age-related term of honor before the family name. These include: *lao* (honorable old one), *xiao* (honorable young one) or occasionally *da* (honorable middle-aged one).

Business

Unless you are good friends or have been asked to do otherwise, you should address your Chinese associates as Miss, Madam, Mr., or by their job title, followed by their family name (Doctor Li, for example). This form of address also applies to company directors, high-ranking officials and teachers. Rarely, if ever, do Chinese use first names on business occasions. And never call anyone "comrade," unless you are a communist also.

Common Chinese Business Titles

(In Government Agencies)

Chinese	English Translation	Usual Seniority	Typical Age Range
Buzhang	Minister	40 years or more	60+
Sizhang, (or)	Department Director (or)	40 years or more	60+
Chuzhang	Section Chief	25 years	45
Kezhang	Office Chief	15 years	35

(In Enterprises)

Chinese	English Translation	Usual Seniority	Typical Age Range
Dongshizhang	Chairman of the Board	40 years or more	60+
Zongjingli	President	40 years or more	60
Fu Zongjingli	Vice President	35 years	55
Bumen Jingli	Department Manager	25 years	45

A title doesn't automatically indicate who is in charge. The person with the real power usually has "vice" or "deputy" in their title, while the top position is often ceremonial. Communist Party officials usually have two business cards. To foreigners, they present themselves as businessmen, while to their countrymen they are, first and foremost, party members.

Chops

The custom of using name chops or seals — characters carved in relief on the bottom of a piece of stone — began during the early Chin Dynasty (about the second century B.C.) as a way of safeguarding government and military correspondence. Once a document had been sealed, a chop would be pressed into a dish of semi-solid red ink (known as "dragon's blood") and pressed on. Hand-carved, chops were almost impossible to forge.

Even today, *danwei* won't accept a document from another *danwei* without the latter's red chop print on it. Many well-to-do Chinese own several chops, in order to foil potential thieves — one to access a bank account, another for contracts. Chops are also used by artists to "sign" paintings and works of calligraphy.

They range from ancient imperial seals weighing several kilograms to small, personal stamps the size of a lipstick. Usually made of jade, marble or soapstone, chops often feature the carving of an animal from the Chinese zodiac at the top.

Shaking Hands

Unlike the Japanese, Chinese do not commonly bow as a form of greeting. Instead, a brief handshake is usual. While meeting elders or senior officials, your handshake should be even more gentle and accompanied by a slight nod.

Sometimes, as an expression of warmth, a Chinese will cover the normal handshake with his left hand. As a sign of respect, Chinese usually lower their eyes slightly when they meet others.

 ## Communication Styles

What's Left Unsaid

Many Westerners find themselves talking too much in China; they can't seem to tolerate silence as well as their Chinese counterparts. The Western concept of "brainstorming" in business meetings, for example, is unknown in China, where everything that is said must be carefully considered in terms of its effect on others and on the consensus-gathering process. Saying whatever comes to mind is considered immature.

Chinese communication is ambiguous, indirect and highly contextual. In conversation, the real meaning, especially if it's negative, is often implied. What has not been said can be as important, or more important, than what has been.

Avoid Saying No

The Chinese use silence as a way to avoid saying "no." Silence also implies, "There are still problems, and we would like to reconsider the main issues."

Another way the Chinese avoid a negative response is to say, "*Yanjiu yanjiu,*" meaning "We will do some research and discuss it later." Don't be too encouraged by the word "research." In many cases, it means "We're not interested." As a foreigner, you can best size up a situation by paying close attention to facial expressions, gestures and overall body language.

Questions

The Chinese standard of what is or is not personal differs from what's considered private information in the West. They will ask directly about your age, your salary, your marital status, and about the price of your clothing, watch or camera. And they're happy to answer such questions about themselves.

However, most Chinese do not openly discuss or ask questions about sexual matters or mores.

The Circuitous Route

One thing you can depend on is that much is accomplished indirectly. A market feasibility study, for example, must often be conducted by engaging Chinese colleagues who utilize their sources.

Until recently, government agencies regarded virtually all business information (including the size, history and annual revenue of a company) as state secrets to be kept from foreigners. Even if such information offered no possible threat, government employees would not risk being accused of the treason of releasing it. The only effective way of obtaining market information had been piece by piece.

Although much has changed, the fear of an unexpected reversal in the government's policies about cooperating with foreigners is not without justification. Giving indirect answers remains a form of self-protection.

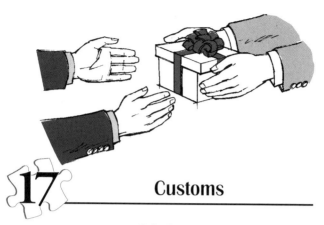

17   Customs

Gift Giving

Chinese do not usually accept a gift, invitation or favor when it is first presented. Politely refusing two or three times is thought to reflect modesty and humility. Accepting something in haste makes a person look aggressive and greedy, as does opening it in front of the giver. Traditionally, the monetary value of a gift indicated the importance of a relationship, but due to increasing contact with foreigners in recent years, the symbolic nature of gifts has taken root.

When you are the recipient, remember that sincerity, appreciation and face (*mianzi*) are far more important than whether or not you accept what's being offered.

Present your gifts with both hands. And when wrapping, be aware that the Chinese ascribe much importance to color. Red is lucky, pink and yellow represent happiness and prosperity; white, grey and black are funeral colors.

If the people you're visiting have requested English-language books or magazines, be discreet about giving them. Materials that are considered anti-communist can get your friends in trouble. If you're visiting relatives, substantial gifts like a radio, television or camera will be appreciated. Other popular items include cigarette lighters, stamps (stamp collecting is a popular hobby), solar-powered calculators and T-shirts with English writing on them. Among the Chinese themselves, popular gift items include health drinks made of "chicken essence" or royal jelly (what worker bees feed to the queen), whiskey, cognac and imported cigarettes.

The following gifts should be avoided:

- White or yellow flowers (especially chrysanthemums), which are used for funerals.

- Pears. The word for "pear" in Chinese sounds the same as "separate" and is considered bad luck.

- Red ink for writing cards or letters. It symbolizes the end of a relationship.

- Clocks of any kind. The word "clock" in Chinese sounds like the expression "the end of life."

Chinese New Year = Everyone's Birthday

Traditionally, the Chinese consider Chinese (Lunar) New Year's Day, as well as the anniversary of their birth, as their birthday. (They also count the time between their conception and birth as a year, so that at birth, they are already one year old.) Birthday foods include *shou mian* (longevity noodles).

On Chinese New Year, it's customary to give *hong bao* ("lucky" money in special red envelopes) to children and to the unmarried offspring of relatives and friends. *Hong bao* are also given to service personnel with whom one deals on a regular basis (housekeepers, baby-sitters). The bills should be new, in even numbers and even amounts, and preferably have sequential serial numbers. Many employers give employees *hong bao* equivalent to a month's salary.

Houses are thoroughly cleaned prior to the new year. (Traditionally, front doors were painted with red lacquer to detract evil spirits, sealed on New Year's Eve, and then broken open the next morning.) It's considered bad luck to walk in old shoes on New Year's Day. In fact, it's traditional to wear an entirely new set of clothes. Because *yu*, the Chinese word for fish, sounds similar to the Chinese word for prosperity, fish is the featured dish in New Year's feasts.

Setting off firecrackers (in order to blow away any bad luck accumulated in the past and bring in good fortune) is a New Year's Eve tradition. In recent years, major cities have, for safety reasons, increasingly restricted the use of firecrackers. As a result, many *da kuan* (wealthy entrepreneurs, literally, "big money") drive out into the countryside to complete this task, thus increasing the likelihood of continued business success in the coming months.

The Power of Numbers

Unlike Taiwanese or people from Hong Kong, most mainland Chinese are not very superstitious about numbers. However, since more than two thirds of China's joint ventures are with Taiwanese or Hong Kong companies, numerology is beginning to have more of an influence.

Five numbers, in particular, have special connotations in business:

- *Si* (four) sounds like "death" in Chinese. Therefore, rather than having a fourth floor, many buildings have floor 3A followed by 3B.

- *Lin* (six) represents luck. It also stands for the six spirits of nature — wind, mountain, river, lightning, moon and sun.

- *Ba* (eight) sounds like *fa* (prosperity), and so is desirable for all occasions.

- *Jiu* (nine) stands for longevity; in ancient times, it could only be used by the Imperial family. The Forbidden City was designed with 9,999 rooms, and the stairs to all palaces have either nine steps or a number that can be divided by nine.

- *Shi san* (thirteen) implies bad luck, just as it does in the West.

Number combinations are also considered significant. *Si ba liu* (four, eight, six), for example, sounds like "to live forever," and *wu jiu ba* (five, nine, eight) is similar to "my prosperity lasts forever."

Acupuncture

This ancient technique is now recognized worldwide as a valuable treatment for everything from migraine headaches and arthritis to hangovers and labor pains during childbirth. Major surgery has been performed using acupuncture alone as the anesthetic.

Three different types of needles, some thinner than a human hair, are inserted into various body points, which the Chinese call meridians. (As many as 2,000 meridians have been identified, though only about 150 are commonly used.) In the past, needles were made from bamboo, gold, silver, copper or tin. Today, only sterilized stainless steel is used.

How acupuncture works is not fully understood by Western science. The meridians are believed to be focal points for internal bodily energy. Somehow, the needles are able to either concentrate that energy into a particular area or to block it (therefore, blocking pain). Many have reported satisfactory results when no other treatment worked.

As in any profession, this one has quacks. Ask a Chinese to recommend a good acupuncturist.

Red and White Events

The two biggest events in Chinese life are weddings and funerals; the traditional color of the former is red, the latter white. In 1949, in an attempt to ban "bourgeois" lifestyles, Mao Zedong banned elaborate "red and white events" (as they're called). But following his death in 1976 and the country's subsequent economic growth, these lavish events have made a comeback

For red events, particularly in the big cities, it's customary for the bride and groom to have their photograph taken in Western-style tuxedos and wedding gowns. Wedding registration is considered a mere formality, but the wedding banquet is a must. These often take place in luxurious restaurants, with anywhere from ten to a hundred round tables, each accommodating eight to ten people, set up for guests. Toasts are plentiful, and after the meal comes *nao dong fang* (literally, "to stir up the bridal chamber"), a tradition of playing practical jokes on the newlyweds.

Funerals (white events) are no less opulent in rural areas, but much less fancy in the cities. Processions begin with several men burning little piles of spirit money (issued by the Bank of Hades) for the dead man to use in Heaven. Buddhist priests in bright yellow robes chant the name of Amitabha Buddha to repel hostile spirits. Large funeral lanterns, marked with the name of the deceased, are followed by a musical ensemble of pipes, woodwinds, flutes, drums, bells, cymbals and gongs.

Some mourners carry offerings to be burned at the graveside — elaborate, custom-made paper replicas of things thought to be of use in the afterlife. These include clothing, automobiles, furniture, television sets, VCRs and even Mercedes Benzes.

Most spectacular of all are the exorcists, who frighten off trespassing, hostile ghosts by dressing up as gods, walking on stilts, doing acrobatics, or juggling as the cortege moves through the streets. Last comes the coffin on a flatbed truck. The most prominent mourners ride with it.

The family of the deceased always hosts a banquet after the funeral to thank their friends. Tradition requires a mourning period of seven weeks, during which family members wear white linen robes.

Such extravagant spectacles are usually reserved for men. It was not long ago that women mourning their husbands were required to walk behind the coffin, as they had walked behind their living husbands, while a husband whose wife had died walked ahead. Funeral banners still sometimes read "faithful and devoted" (*qing xin*) for a man, but "chaste and submissive" (*zhen shun*) for a woman.

Dress & Appearance

Clothing styles in China are changing rapidly. The uniform-like, unisex Mao jacket has almost disappeared in big cities. Stylish, colorful Chinese fashions may cost a local person one or two months' salary. Many Chinese men wear Western-style suits with ties.

Jeans are acceptable informal wear for both sexes. For sight-seeing, dresses and skirts are preferable to pants or shorts. Rubber-soled shoes are recommended for visiting factories, communes and the like, where the walks are likely to be long and the floors rough.

Both for business meetings and entertainment, loud colors and showy jewelry should be avoided. Women should also avoid low necklines, mini skirts, and solid red or white dresses (as previously mentioned, red is reserved for brides and white for funerals).

Reading the Chinese

Chinese gestures and body language can be incomprehensible to Westerners. Here are some general guidelines.

- **Physical Contact**

Lightly touching another person's arm when speaking is a sign of close familiarity. Except for shaking hands, do not touch anyone unless you know them very well. Any public physical contact between opposite genders, including married couples, used to be unacceptable. Today, however, it's common in big cities, especially among young people. Chinese do not hug or kiss when meeting or saying good-bye. But people of the same sex can be seen holding hands as a gesture of friendship.

Women should be careful not to brush against a monk or Buddhist priest (they are forbidden to touch women). Flirting or any other behavior that can be interpreted as violating China's strict moral code can get you expelled from the country. However, be aware that pushing and shoving on buses and trains is normal. Apologies are usually not offered.

The safest nonverbal tactic to employ is smiling.

- **Eye Contact and Facial Expression**

Chinese will often avoid eye contact during

conversations, especially when talking to the opposite sex or to strangers. Traditionally, it was considered impolite and aggressive to look directly into another's eyes while talking. However, outside of the big cities, foreigners may be the subject of stares, especially if they are blond or red-headed.

Chinese typically have a "blank" facial expression during introductions. This is not a sign of unhappiness, dissatisfaction, or unfriendliness, but reflects the belief that there is virtue in concealing emotions.

- **Social Distance**

Westerners typically stand about a meter apart, while Chinese are more comfortable at a lesser distance. If you move away, your Chinese associates will move with you until you're backed against a wall. If you're uncomfortable, try sitting down.

- **Truth and Courtesy**

Chinese will sometimes tell their foreign guests whatever they believe they want to hear, whether it's true or not. To minimize risk, use other resources to double- or triple-check the reliability of what you've been told.

- **Humor**

Humor is perfectly acceptable in informal situations, but you should refrain from making jokes when speaking to a group, especially on formal occasions. Sexual jokes are taboo. Humor doesn't often translate well across cultures. Puns are impossible, and jokes concerning persons or events specific to your own country are not likely to be understood.

Chinese smile as a courtesy when they realize that you are making a joke, whether or not they have understood it. You should do the same.

- **Body Language**

In China, posture indicates class, education and breeding. In meetings, sit straight in a chair with both feet on the floor. Don't slouch or cross your legs in the Western fashion. Never point to anyone with a finger or use your head or foot to refer to someone. The Chinese gesture for "come here" is to extend one arm with the hand palm down and move your fingers in a scratching motion. Using the thumb and index finger to form a circle to symbolize "OK" is unknown. "Thumbs up" has the same meaning in the East as in the West.

The common gesture of shrugging the shoulders does not mean "I don't know." Chinese interpret this as disdainful and disrespectful. Nodding the head up and down indicates agreement, and shaking from side to side, disagreement. However, nodding the head can also simply indicate acknowledgment. Holding your hand up in front of you and waving it from side to side also means "no."

Applause has the same meaning in China as in the West. But in China, the people being applauded often clap back to show their appreciation.

On public streets, spitting and blowing one's nose without benefit of a handkerchief are fairly common. They are regarded as ridding the body of waste.

Subjects of Conversation

- **Family**
  The Chinese may try to evaluate you as the member of a family as well as an individual. Asking questions about associates' families is natural and acceptable.

  However, there is disagreement among the Chinese about the government's one-child policy; avoid expressing opinions about family size.

- **Sexual Orientation**
  The Chinese are puzzled and often judgmental about what they see as immorality. Discussions of

alternative life-styles and sexual orientations will not be well received. In the unlikely event that a Chinese expresses a strong opinion about such matters, it's probably best to change the subject rather than disagree.

• **Politics**

Avoid political discussions and don't criticize the government, even if a Chinese initiates such a conversation. Don't make comparisons between China and Taiwan; the Chinese consider Taiwan one of their provinces.

The 1989 Tian'anmen Square incident and other human rights issues are taboo, as is the situation in Tibet. The "Cultural Revolution," now considered ancient history, may come up in conversation; although some Chinese are willing to discuss that turbulent time freely, and even to relate personal stories, others are saddened or shamed by their memories.

Do not criticize either your own or other countries. It will make the Chinese uncomfortable.

• **Money**

It's not uncommon to be asked how much money you make. Avoid this topic, when possible, with work partners — knowing that you make twenty times as much as they do can cause resentment. One way to downplay Western incomes is to compare the purchasing power in China with your home country. This may be better understood than a solid salary figure, which may seem astronomical when converted into Chinese currency.

Entertaining: The Banquet Tradition

20

Businesspeople, journalists and others staying in China for long periods of time are often housed in protected compounds. If a Chinese is invited for dinner, even with a printed invitation, he or she may be questioned by the authorities and have their name taken; therefore, it's likely that they will turn down the offer. Most Chinese will feel more comfortable being invited to a foreigner's home with a group.

Dining in a Chinese home is a mark of special favor, and it may take several years before such an invitation is extended. Staying overnight in a Chinese home used to be forbidden but is now possible with a registration permit from a local police station.

If you want to meet a friend, it's best to do so in a restaurant.

Exotic Culinary Fare

A Chinese proverb says that "for the people, food is heaven." Anything is fair game for the *wok*. Dishes like cobra or python soup, stir-fried scorpions, bird's nests, shark's fin soup, bear paw stew and marinated camel hooves are believed to build up inner energy, and even to enhance the diner's immune system. Many of these recipes probably date back to a time when food was scarce and people made do as best they could. Today, they are expensive and highly prized.

Dog meat is sometimes served (in the south, a breed called Zhou is a particular delicacy), along with deer and rabbit, all of which are believed to enhance circulation and so are often served in winter.

Since it's the Chinese custom to offer what they think is the finest fare to their guests, they will be delighted if you are willing to try them but will not be surprised if you decline.

(Of course, what's exotic depends on your frame of reference. Three of the most popular restaurants among locals in Beijing are McDonald's, Kentucky Fried Chicken and Pizza Hut.)

Dim Sum

The Guangdong area specializes in *dim sum* (literally, "little hearts"). Usually served until mid-afternoon, these delicate rice-dough pastries, similar to Western appetizers, are filled with meats, vegetables and shellfish. Some are steamed, others are deep fried. When you're finished eating, the waiter will count the number of little plates on your table and calculate the bill accordingly.

Dim sum runs the gamut from *cha shao bao* (steamed buns filled with barbecued pork), *xia jiao* (translucent, shrimp-stuffed dumplings) and succulent crab claws (in fancier teahouses) to turnip or taro root cakes, marinated chicken wrapped in foil, and duck feet steamed in ginger. Sweet, flaky-crusted custard tarts are popular for dessert.

The Banquet Begins

Banquets are usually held in restaurants in private rooms, either for dinner or lunch. As in all other situations, the head of your delegation should enter the room first. If you are met with a round of applause from the Chinese, smile, nod slightly at them and applaud back.

At a formal dinner, the principal host and guest are seated facing each other, with the latter facing the door and the host with his back to the door. On less formal occasions, the host assumes the seat facing the door, with the guest at his immediate right. Other guests are seated in descending order of rank around the table. Guests should always wait to be guided to their places and should not sit until the principal host and guest have done so.

Banquets usually contain four main courses: *leng pen* (cold dishes), *re chao* (hot stir-fries that often alternate between crisp and tender and between sweet/sour and spicy), *da cai* (often a whole cooked fish, symbolizing abundance) and *tang* (soup). Try to pace yourself. Ten or twelve courses are common, and it's bad form to finish eating before they've all been served. Many meat dishes contain small bones (use chopsticks to remove them from your mouth, not fingers).

Roast Peking Duck (*Beijing Kaoya*) is a northern speciality. Platters of duck meat and crispy skin are served with thin pancakes, *hai xian* sauce and scallion "brushes." The duck carcass is cooked into a soup stock with wintermelon or cabbage and served as the following course.

The serving of fruit signals the end of the meal. In China, fruit is symbolic: oranges for happiness, pomegranates for fertility, apples for peace, pears for prosperity and peaches for immortality.

Gan Bei

At the beginning of a business banquet, the principal Chinese host will usually propose a toast. Though much of what is stated may be superficial, it will also reflect the general tone established at the first business meeting. The toast always ends with the expression, *"gan bei"* ("bottoms up"). You're not obliged to empty your glass in one swallow, but you'll be showered with praise if you do. The principal guest is then expected to propose a counter-toast.

Maotai, a wicked 120-proof sorghum-based liquor, is traditional for banquet toasts. Or you might try *Shao xing*, a red rice wine. Local beers are very good and usually served warm. A courteous host will try to get his guests drunk. The Chinese say, "When the wine is in, the truth is out," and a relationship will certainly get warmer after a few drinks.

The Chinese don't usually talk about serious business over meals. Instead, they take the opportunity to deepen personal relationships. History, scenery sights, culture, arts, tradition and inquiries about the health of the other's family are good topics. However, a generous infusion of alcohol may elicit "real opinions" about political and social issues that you will not hear on other occasions. It's best not to involve yourself in conversations on sensitive subjects. Drinking also presents an opportunity for personal questions, so be prepared. If you're uncomfortable with a particular inquiry, try some humor to get off the hook, such as, "I've promised my father to keep it a secret."

Generally speaking, women in China do not drink alcoholic beverages. Visiting businesswomen who are offered a drink are advised to accept it, take a sip, and then leave it.

Using Chopsticks

Although mastering chopsticks isn't mandatory, using them reflects an interest in the culture. One way to practice is to pick up peanuts one at a time and put them in your mouth. When you can do this with relative ease, you should have no trouble at a banquet.

The following protocol applies:

- When the chopsticks are not in use, they should be placed on the table horizontally next to your plate or on the chopstick rest (if there is one).

- Use the porcelain spoon, not chopsticks, to eat the vegetables or meat in the soup. The Chinese prefer porcelain to metal because it doesn't absorb heat and has no metallic taste.

- Don't gesture with chopsticks in your hand.

- In some parts of China, dropping your chopsticks is considered bad luck.

- Use serving spoons, if they are provided, to pick up food from communal plates. Otherwise, turn your chopsticks around, and use the blunt ends.

- Never stick your chopsticks straight up in a rice bowl. It reminds the Chinese of temple incense burned in memory of their ancestors.

Banquet Gifts

At the banquet, you will probably be presented with a gift. For men, silk ties are typical; for women, silk scarves. If you're in China on business, bring gifts for your Chinese associates — something associated with your company (a calendar, a high-quality pen with your firm's name or logo on it, or a book of photographs of the area where your company is located) is always appropriate.

Expensive gifts may cause personal embarrassment and political or social awkwardness, and it's best to give the same thing to everyone. If your gifts vary, give the most expensive one to the leader of the Chinese team; always present it to him first, and then to the others in descending order of seniority.

Smoking

Many Chinese smoke cigarettes, and since knowledge about the effects of second-hand smoke is quite low, smoking in public areas is common in China. It's acceptable for women to smoke at banquets and parties, and in private, but not elsewhere.

It is perfectly acceptable to decline an invitation to light up, but it would be considered rude for you to ask a Chinese not to smoke during a banquet or meeting. If at all possible, bear with it. If you do smoke, it's customary to offer cigarettes to others before lighting up yourself.

The Check and Tipping

Financial transactions have usually been arranged beforehand. Sincere appreciation should be expressed, but inquiries about paying or sharing the bill will offend the host. Consider hosting a banquet of your own as a way to reciprocate.

Tipping is a Western tradition, and until fifteen or so years ago, it was widely regarded as a filthy capitalist ploy to bribe the proletariat. Times have changed in China, and although gratuities are still thought to conflict with the moral standard, the staff will not be insulted if you discreetly offer a tip for exemplary service. In most cities, 15 percent of the total restaurant bill will be automatically added on as a "service fee", regardless of customer satisfaction. In big cities such as Beijing, Shanghai and Guangzhou, tipping taxi drivers, tour guides and hotel service staff is common.

21 Socializing

Traditionally, foreign visitors have been disappointed with China's night life. However, if you have an opportunity to attend a local acrobatic or magic troupe, by all means do. Their talent will astonish you.

Until very recently, socializing for business purposes was considered appropriate only for high-ranking officials who had to deal with visiting diplomats. But this is changing with the growing number of international companies that hold functions for their employees, families and friends. In fact, social gatherings have become so popular among Chinese that they have adopted the English word "party" into their vocabulary (there being no Mandarin term for such an event).

Karaoke

By tradition and nature, for a Chinese who is not a professional entertainer to perform in front of his peers would be embarrassing and immodest. But karaoke clubs, a recent import from Japan, provide a socially acceptable way to display one's talent. Karaoke means "empty orchestra" in Japanese. The

clubs feature a raised platform, a standing micro-
phone and music videos that depict a song's story
with the lyrics displayed at the bottom of the screen.

To be invited to sing karaoke is a sign of acceptance; it means that the Chinese are willing to reveal
more of themselves to you. And it's an excellent way
to establish closer relations. Ignorance of Chinese
music will not save you — most clubs have American
songs in their repertoire ("My Way" and "Yesterday"
are very popular). No matter how poor your attempt,
it will be greeted with much praise and applause.

La Scala a la Beijing

Next to temples and festivals, classical local
opera offers one of the most spectacular images of
China's culture. High-pitched violins, thumping
drums, whining flutes, clanging gongs, elaborate
costumes, daring acrobatics, and deftly mimed
movement are all designed to overwhelm the audience's senses. The themes are drawn from folklore,
ancient legends, and historical events as familiar to
the average Chinese as the Greek myths and tales
of King Arthur's court are to Westerners.

The opera's most prominent theatrical device is
facial decoration, which is believed to have originated during the T'ang Dynasty (7th century A.D.).
The face paint colors help to distinguish heroes from
villains and gods. Red indicates loyalty and honesty;
white represents cunning (often a criminal or a
clown); blue is for bravery (and characters with wild
personalities); black means honest and dignified
(like a judge or general); yellow shows intelligence
and reserve; brown means strong and stubborn;
green indicates either a ghost or a demon; and gold
is reserved for gods and benevolent spirits.

If the performance takes place in a teahouse
(rather than in a formal theatre), don't be surprised

if most of the audience shows up late and munches watermelon seeds, talks loudly or smokes during the performance. The Chinese know all the stories by heart and all the actors by reputation and so are usually silent only during the most popular scenes and arias.

Gambling: A Cultural Phenomenon

The Chinese addiction to gambling dates back to antiquity — a lottery helped finance the building of the Great Wall. Although the Communist Party denounces gambling as one of the "five evils" to be stamped out (along with feasting, drinking, prostitution and drug use), crap tables, electronic poker arcades and underground casinos abound. Bets are exchanged over everything from sports to fighting songbirds.

Ma jiang (mahjong) is a particular favorite. Possibly invented by boatmen along China's rivers, the game is played with rectangular tiles by two to four people, and played at an astonishing speed. Winning or losing thousands of *yuan* in a night is not unusual.

In Guangzhou, shaggy Mongolian ponies race toward the finish line at the race track. Since this is the People's Republic, the term "betting" has been replaced with the less bourgeois "intelligence competition" — that is, the challenge of making superior guesses.

Officially, the uneven distribution of wealth is considered an example of capitalist exploitation and cultural corruption. But in China, where being lucky means securing favor with the gods, the love of gambling seems to override loyalties to political ideology.

22 Basic Mandarin Phrases

English	Chinese (pinyin)	Pronunciation
Yes	*Dui*	*Doo-ee*
No	*Bu dui*	*Boo doo-ee*
Please	*Qing*	*Ching*
Sorry; excuse me	*Dui bu qi*	*Doo-ee boo chee*
Hello		
(on phone)	*Wei*	*Wei*
(in person)	*Ni hao*	*Knee how*
How are you?	*Ni hao ma?*	*Knee how mah*
My name is__	*Wo jiao__*	*Wah jee-oh__*
Thank you	*Xie xie*	*Shee-yeh shee-yeh*
You're welcome	*Bu xie*	*Boo shee-yeh*
Good-bye	*Zai jian*	*Dzye jee-en*
I don't understand	*Wo bu dong*	*Wah boo dong*
How much?	*Duo shao qian?*	*Doo-oh shah-oh*

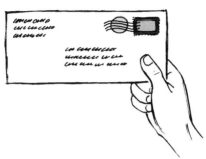

 Correspondence

The order of a Chinese mailing address is the opposite of a Western one. A letter addressed in English to:

Mr. Weiqiang Zhang
The Ministry of Chemistry
Bureau of Technology
Jianguo Menwai, Fuwai Dajie 88
Beijing, 100080
China

would be addressed in Chinese to:

China
Beijing, 100080
Jianguo Menwai, Fuwai Dajie 88
Huagong Bu, Jishu Si
Zhang Weiqiang (notice the surname goes first)

Don't use red ink to write cards or letters. Though generally an auspicious color, in correspondence it symbolizes the end of a relationship.

You may wish to travel with a glue stick or roll of transparent tape, as Chinese envelopes and stamps don't have adhesive on them.

24 Useful Numbers

- International access code from China 00
- China Country Code .... [86]
- City codes: Beijing .... (10)
  Shanghai .... (21)
  Guangzhou .... (20)
- Emergency numbers in China
  Police 110
  Fire .... (119)
  Ambulance .... (120)
- Directory Assistance in China
  Local 113
  Long Distance 114
  Hong Kong & Macau 115
- Public Security Bureau (visas, travel permits)
  Beijing .... (10) 6512-2471
  Shanghai .... (20) 6321-5380
- Sino-German Poli-Clinic (English-speaking doctors)
  Beijing .... (10) 6501-1983
- International Medical Ctr. Beijing (10) 6465-1561
- Tourist Info (CITS)
  Beijing .... (10) 6515-8570
  Shanghai .... (20) 6321-7200
- Air China (domestic flights) .... (10) 6601-3336
  (international flights) .... (10) 6601-6667

 Books & Internet Addresses

China Pop: How Soap Opera, Tabloids and Best-sellers Are Transforming a Culture by Jianying Zha. The New Press, New York, USA, 1995. A highly original look at how China is being reshaped by media, consumerism, and a new generation of Chinese artists and entrepreneurs.

China Business, The Portable Encyclopedia for Doing Business With China, by Christine Genzberger et al. World Trade Press, Novato, California USA. An encyclopedic view of doing business in and with China. Part of the World Trade Press Country Business Guide Series.

The Great Wall in Ruins: Communication and Cultural Change in China by Godwin C. Chu and Yanan Ju. State University of New York Press, Albany, New York, USA, 1993. An overview of the effects of recent social and economic changes on China's culture and communications.

China: Business Strategies for the '90s by Arne J. De Keijzer. Pacific View Press, Berkeley, California, USA, 1992. Based on case studies, this book offers planning, negotiation and investment strategies for foreigners.

China: A New History by John K. Fairbank. Harvard University Press, Boston, Massachusetts, USA, 1993. This longtime China expert and scholar offers new insights into the development of China.

Internet Addresses

China Business Vista
www.chinavista.com
(Yellow pages, news, trade, investment)
Business China
www.business-china.com
(products, companies, foreign investment, finance, business services, jobs, business directory)
China Online
www.chinaonline.com
(news, analysis, business information)
China Business Directory
www.china-business-directory.com
(over 10,000 business listings)
China Today
www.chinatoday.com
(arts, humanities, culture, education, entertainment, finance, health, government, history, investment, law, travel and more)
China Business Review
www.chinabusinessreview.com
(official magazine of the US-China Business Council)
The Great Web of China
www.comnex.com/
(Comprehensive information about travel, the Shanghai stock market, investment opportunities and upcoming business events)
China Travel
www.chinatour.com/

Jenny Li is a national of the People's Republic of China and the daughter of Yaming Kuang, one of China's most renowned Confucian thinkers and educators. An MBA in international business, she conducts market research for U.S. companies entering China and serves as a management consultant for Chinese-American joint ventures. She has lived in the United States since 1986.